Understanding Suicide: Prevention, Awareness, and Moving Forward

C. P. Kumar

Reiki Healer

Roorkee - 247667, India

Disclaimer

While every effort has been made to ensure the accuracy and completeness of the content in this book, the author cannot guarantee that the information contained herein is error-free, up-to-date, or suitable for every individual circumstance.

The author shall not be held liable or responsible for any errors or omissions in the content of the book, nor for any damages, or losses that may arise from any actions taken based upon the suggestions or contents presented in the book.

Readers are advised to use their own judgment and discretion in applying the information provided in this book, and to consult with qualified professionals before taking any action based on the contents of this book. The author disclaims any and all liability or responsibility for any actions taken or not taken based on the information contained in this book.

DEDICATION

To all those whose lives have been touched by suicide,

This book is dedicated to you – the survivors, the fighters, the advocates, and the supporters. Your resilience and strength in the face of unimaginable pain inspire us to shed light on the dark shadows surrounding suicide.

To those we have lost to suicide, you are deeply missed. Your lives were not defined by this tragic act, but by the love, joy, and potential you brought into the world. We carry your memory in our hearts as a reminder of the urgent need to understand and prevent this devastating outcome.

To the individuals and families who have experienced the profound aftermath of suicide, we recognize your pain and sorrow. Through this book, we hope to provide solace, knowledge, and practical guidance to navigate the complex journey of healing and recovery.

To the mental health professionals, researchers, and organizations tirelessly working to prevent suicide, your dedication and commitment are commendable. Your unwavering efforts to enhance awareness, develop effective strategies, and provide support to those in need are invaluable in this collective fight against suicide.

To the communities around the world, we stand united in our resolve to address the multifaceted factors contributing to suicide. By understanding the social, cultural, economic, and psychological influences, we strive to create environments that foster mental well-being, inclusivity, and compassion.

To those who are struggling, know that you are not alone. This book seeks to provide you with a roadmap for identifying warning signs, accessing resources, and finding hope in the darkest moments. We believe in your resilience and offer our unwavering support.

Finally, this book is dedicated to the pursuit of a future where suicide is no longer an option for those in despair. By cultivating empathy, fostering dialogue, and implementing evidence-based strategies, we can forge a path towards a society that values mental health and embraces the power of prevention.

Together, let us honor the lives touched by suicide, and may this dedication serve as a beacon of hope, understanding, and progress for all.

With heartfelt dedication,

C. P. Kumar

CONTENTS

PREFACE

Suicide is a deeply sensitive and complex issue that demands our unwavering attention. It is a global phenomenon that affects individuals, families, and communities, leaving behind a wake of grief and unanswered questions. In the face of such a profound challenge, it becomes crucial for us to deepen our understanding, explore prevention strategies, and foster awareness.

"Understanding Suicide: Prevention, Awareness, and Moving Forward" seeks to delve into the intricate layers of suicide, providing a comprehensive exploration of its causes, warning signs, and the factors that contribute to its prevalence. This book aims to shed light on the relationship between mental health and suicide, examining the role of substance abuse, social, cultural, and economic influences, as well as other pertinent aspects.

Recognizing the immense impact of suicide on different age groups, from adolescents and young adults to the elderly, this book addresses the unique challenges faced by each demographic. It highlights the importance of early identification and intervention, empowering readers with the knowledge to identify the warning signs and support at-risk individuals.

Moreover, this book acknowledges the lasting effects of suicide on family and friends, examining the emotional toll and providing guidance on navigating the healing process. It emphasizes the need for compassionate support systems and highlights the invaluable role of mental health professionals in suicide prevention.

As we strive to cultivate a society that understands and supports those in need, this book explores the ethics surrounding suicide from diverse cultural and religious perspectives. It encourages open dialogue and promotes empathy, understanding that our beliefs and values shape our understanding of this complex issue.

In addition, this book sheds light on the specific risk factors faced by certain groups, such as members of the LGBTQ+ community. By examining their unique challenges, it offers insights into tailored approaches to prevention and support.

Given the prevalence of cyberbullying in the digital age, this book underscores the connection between online harassment and suicide rates. It emphasizes the urgent need for proactive measures to combat cyberbullying and create a safe environment for vulnerable individuals.

Furthermore, this book recognizes the impact of the global COVID-19 pandemic on mental health and suicide rates worldwide. By providing a global perspective, it underscores the importance of prioritizing mental well-being and resilience in our collective response to future crises.

"Understanding Suicide: Prevention, Awareness, and Moving Forward" aspires to be a valuable resource for mental health professionals, educators, policymakers, families, and individuals seeking a deeper understanding of suicide and its prevention. It is our hope that this book will foster dialogue, break stigmas, and guide efforts towards a world where every life is cherished and suicide is prevented.

Together, let us embark on this journey of understanding, awareness, and action. By arming ourselves with knowledge and compassion, we can work towards a future where suicide rates decline, and lives are saved.

C. P. Kumar
Reiki Healer
Former Scientist 'G', National Institute of Hydrology
Roorkee - 247667, India
E-mail: cpkumar@yahoo.com
Web: https://www.angelfire.com/nh/cpkumar/virgo.html

Introduction

Suicide is a deeply concerning issue that affects individuals, families, and communities worldwide. It is a tragic act involving intentional self-harm leading to death. Understanding the concept of suicide and its prevalence is crucial to address this public health crisis effectively. This article aims to define suicide and explore its prevalence, shedding light on the factors contributing to this distressing phenomenon.

What is Suicide?

Suicide refers to the act of intentionally causing one's death. It involves a deliberate action, such as self-inflicted harm or the ingestion of substances with lethal intent. Suicide is often associated with mental health conditions, such as depression, anxiety disorders, bipolar disorder, or substance abuse. However, it is essential to recognize that not all individuals who die by suicide have a diagnosed mental illness.

Suicide Prevalence

1. Global Perspective

Suicide is a global public health concern, affecting countries across the world. According to the World Health Organization (WHO), suicide accounts for approximately 800,000 deaths annually, making it the second leading cause of death among individuals aged 15 to 29 years. The global suicide rate is estimated to be around 10.5 per 100,000 population.

2. Regional Variations

Suicide rates vary significantly between regions. High-income countries, particularly in Europe, have relatively lower suicide rates compared to low- and middle-income countries. However, within countries, there may be regional variations, with some areas experiencing higher suicide rates than others. It is important to consider these variations when implementing prevention strategies.

Factors Contributing to Suicide

1. Mental Health Conditions

Mental health conditions play a significant role in suicide. Many individuals who die by suicide have experienced depression, anxiety, or other mental illnesses. These conditions can contribute to feelings of hopelessness, despair, and a sense of being a burden to others, leading to suicidal thoughts.

2. Substance Abuse

Substance abuse, including alcohol and drug addiction, is closely linked to suicide. Substance abuse can impair judgment, exacerbate mental health conditions, and increase impulsivity, making individuals more susceptible to suicidal behaviors.

3. Social Factors

Social factors, such as isolation, loneliness, and a lack of social support, can contribute to suicide risk. People who feel disconnected from their families, friends, or communities may be more vulnerable to suicidal ideation. Other factors, including a history of trauma, childhood abuse, or a family history of suicide, can also increase the risk.

4. Access to Lethal Means

The availability and accessibility of lethal means, such as firearms, pesticides, or medications, can significantly impact suicide rates. Restricting access to these means has been shown to reduce suicide rates, highlighting the importance of implementing effective means restriction policies.

Suicide Prevention

Preventing suicide requires a multifaceted approach that addresses individual, community, and societal factors. Some key strategies include:

1. Mental Health Promotion

Promoting mental health and well-being is crucial in preventing suicide. This involves increasing awareness, reducing stigma surrounding mental health, and providing accessible and affordable mental health services.

2. Early Intervention and Treatment

Early identification and intervention for mental health conditions can prevent suicidal behaviors. Providing timely access to mental health care and evidence-based treatments is essential in reducing suicide risk.

3. Means Restriction

Implementing policies and interventions to restrict access to lethal means can significantly reduce suicide rates. This may involve stricter gun control laws, safer packaging of medications, or reducing access to highly toxic substances.

4. Enhancing Support Systems

Creating supportive environments that foster social connections and provide emotional support can help individuals at risk. Building strong community networks, promoting social integration, and improving access to crisis helplines and support groups are vital in suicide prevention.

Conclusion

Suicide is a complex and multifaceted issue that requires comprehensive efforts to address its prevalence effectively. By understanding the factors contributing to suicide and implementing prevention strategies, we can work towards reducing its incidence and providing support for individuals struggling with suicidal thoughts. Promoting mental health, early intervention, means restriction, and strengthening support systems are essential steps towards preventing suicide and creating a safer, more compassionate society.

Introduction

Mental health is a crucial aspect of overall well-being, encompassing emotional, psychological, and social well-being. It affects how individuals think, feel, and act, and plays a significant role in determining how people handle stress, make choices, and relate to others. Unfortunately, when mental health conditions are left unaddressed or misunderstood, they can lead to severe consequences, including suicide. This article aims to explore the connection between mental health and suicide, shedding light on the importance of understanding and addressing mental health issues.

The Prevalence of Mental Health Issues

Mental health issues are far more prevalent than most people realize. According to the World Health Organization (WHO), approximately 1 in 4 people worldwide will experience a mental health condition at some point in their lives. These conditions can range from common disorders such as depression and anxiety to more severe conditions like bipolar disorder and schizophrenia. Despite their prevalence, mental health issues often go unnoticed or untreated, which can contribute to an increased risk of suicide.

Mental Health and Suicide: The Complex Relationship

Suicide is a tragic outcome of untreated or poorly managed mental health conditions. While not all individuals with mental health issues will experience suicidal thoughts or engage in self-harming behaviors, the risk is significantly higher compared to the general population. Several factors contribute to the complex relationship between mental health and suicide:

1. Untreated Mental Health Conditions: When mental health conditions are left untreated or undiagnosed, they can worsen over time, increasing the risk of suicidal ideation. Lack of access to mental health services, social stigma, or denial of the problem are common barriers to seeking help.

2. Co-occurring Disorders: Mental health conditions often coexist with other disorders such as substance abuse, eating disorders, or personality disorders. The presence of multiple conditions can intensify emotional distress, leading to an increased risk of suicide.

3. Hopelessness and Despair: Prolonged emotional suffering, feelings of hopelessness, and a lack of perceived solutions can make individuals vulnerable to suicidal thoughts. When mental health issues are severe or chronic, individuals may struggle to envision a way out of their pain, leading them to consider suicide as an escape.

4. Social Isolation: Mental health conditions can significantly impact an individual's ability to connect with others and maintain healthy relationships. Social isolation and a lack of support networks can exacerbate feelings of loneliness and contribute to suicidal thoughts.

Recognizing Warning Signs and Risk Factors

To effectively address the connection between mental health and suicide, it is crucial to recognize the warning signs and risk factors associated with suicide. While each person's experience is unique, some common indicators include:

1. Verbal Cues: Expressing thoughts of suicide, feeling trapped, being a burden to others, or having no reason to live.

2. Behavioral Changes: Withdrawing from social activities, giving away possessions, engaging in risky behaviors, or displaying extreme mood swings.

3. Emotional Instability: Intense sadness, anger, or irritability, feeling hopeless or humiliated, or experiencing a loss of interest in previously enjoyed activities.

4. Changes in Sleep and Appetite: Insomnia, hypersomnia, significant weight loss or gain, or changes in eating habits.

Addressing Mental Health and Preventing Suicide

To effectively address the connection between mental health and suicide, it is crucial to take proactive steps in supporting individuals experiencing mental health issues. Here are some essential strategies:

1. Promoting Mental Health Education: Creating awareness and providing education about mental health conditions, their symptoms, and available resources is vital in reducing stigma and encouraging early intervention.

2. Enhancing Access to Mental Health Services: Governments, organizations, and communities must prioritize mental health services, ensuring they are accessible, affordable, and inclusive. This includes increasing the number of mental health professionals and expanding mental health coverage in insurance plans.

3. Encouraging Open Dialogue: Foster a culture that encourages open conversations about mental health, providing safe spaces for individuals to express their emotions and seek support without fear of judgment.

4. Supporting Individuals at Risk: Establish support networks and crisis helplines to assist individuals in crisis, providing them with immediate support and connecting them to appropriate resources.

5. Empowering Peer Support: Peer support programs play a crucial role in mental health recovery. Encouraging the development of support groups and peer counseling services can provide individuals with a sense of belonging and understanding.

Conclusion

Understanding the connection between mental health and suicide is vital in preventing the tragic loss of life. By promoting mental health education, enhancing access to mental health services, encouraging open dialogue, and supporting individuals at risk, we can create a society that prioritizes mental well-being. Remember, mental health conditions are treatable, and recovery is possible. By providing understanding, support, and resources, we can make a positive impact and save lives.

Introduction

Suicide is a tragic and complex issue that affects individuals and communities worldwide. It is important to understand the various factors that contribute to suicide in order to develop effective prevention strategies. This article will explore the social, cultural, and economic influences that play a significant role in increasing the risk of suicide.

Social Factors

1. Social Isolation

One of the key social factors contributing to suicide is social isolation. When individuals lack meaningful social connections, they may feel lonely, disconnected, and unsupported, which can exacerbate feelings of hopelessness and despair.

2. Relationship Problems

Difficulties in personal relationships, such as marital problems, family conflicts, or the loss of a loved one, can significantly contribute to suicidal ideation. These challenges can create intense emotional distress and a sense of helplessness, increasing the risk of suicide.

3. Bullying and Stigma

Experiencing bullying or being subjected to social stigma can have devastating effects on mental health. Victims of bullying or individuals facing discrimination based on their gender identity, sexual orientation, race, or other characteristics may feel marginalized, leading to a higher risk of suicide.

Cultural Factors

1. Cultural Norms and Beliefs

Cultural norms and beliefs surrounding mental health and suicide can influence individuals' attitudes and behaviors. In some cultures, there may be stigma associated with seeking help for mental health issues, leading individuals to suffer in silence and avoid seeking support.

2. Honor and Shame

Certain cultures place a significant emphasis on honor and shame, which can contribute to the risk of suicide. When individuals face situations that they perceive as bringing shame or dishonor to themselves or their families, they may resort to suicide as a way to restore their perceived honor or avoid the shame.

3. Religious and Spiritual Factors

Religious and spiritual beliefs can both serve as protective factors and contribute to suicide risk. While faith and religious communities can provide support, comfort, and hope, rigid religious beliefs or perceived moral conflicts may exacerbate feelings of guilt and hopelessness, increasing the risk of suicide.

Economic Factors

1. Unemployment and Financial Strain

Economic difficulties, such as unemployment, poverty, and financial strain, can significantly impact mental health and increase the risk of suicide. The stress of financial instability and the inability to meet basic needs can lead to feelings of despair and hopelessness.

2. Income Inequality

Societies with high levels of income inequality tend to have higher suicide rates. The perception of inequity and a lack of opportunities for social mobility can contribute to feelings of despair and hopelessness among individuals who feel trapped in their socioeconomic circumstances.

3. Access to Lethal Means

Easy access to lethal means, such as firearms or certain medications, is a critical economic factor in suicide. Availability and accessibility of such means can increase the likelihood of impulsive acts and reduce the time for intervention, significantly impacting suicide rates.

Conclusion

Suicide is a complex issue influenced by a combination of social, cultural, and economic factors. Understanding and addressing these factors is crucial for effective suicide prevention efforts. By promoting social connections, combating stigma, fostering cultural sensitivity, providing economic opportunities, and ensuring restricted access to lethal means, we can work towards creating a supportive and safe environment that reduces the risk of suicide and promotes mental well-being for all individuals.

Introduction

Suicide is a global public health concern, affecting individuals of all ages, genders, and backgrounds. It is crucial to understand and recognize the warning signs associated with suicide to help identify those who may be at risk. By being aware of these signs, we can take preventive measures and provide support to individuals who are struggling. This article aims to shed light on the warning signs of suicide and the importance of identifying at-risk individuals.

Understanding the Scope of Suicide

Suicide is a complex issue influenced by various factors, including mental health conditions, social isolation, previous suicide attempts, substance abuse, and life stressors. It is a leading cause of death worldwide, and its prevention requires a multidimensional approach that includes early identification and intervention.

Changes in Behavior and Mood

One of the primary indicators of suicidal ideation is a noticeable change in behavior and mood. Keep an eye out for the following warning signs:

1. Withdrawal and Isolation: Individuals contemplating suicide often withdraw from social interactions, preferring solitude over engaging with others.

2. Persistent Sadness: Unexplained or prolonged sadness, feelings of hopelessness, and an overall sense of despair can be signs of underlying suicidal thoughts.

3. Drastic Mood Swings: Frequent and extreme mood swings, from high energy to profound sadness or irritability, can be a red flag.

4. Increased Irritability and Aggression: Suicidal individuals may exhibit heightened irritability, impatience, or aggressive behavior, which can be out of character for them.

Verbal and Non-Verbal Cues

Communication is key when it comes to identifying individuals at risk of suicide. Pay attention to the following verbal and non-verbal cues:

1. Verbal Hints: Expressions of feeling trapped, being a burden to others, having no reason to live, or talking about death and dying should not be taken lightly.

2. Expressions of Hopelessness: Feelings of hopelessness and a belief that things will never get better are strong indicators of suicidal ideation.

3. Giving Away Belongings: Suicidal individuals may start giving away their possessions as a way to say goodbye or ease the burden on loved ones.

4. Sudden Improvement: Paradoxically, a sudden improvement in mood and demeanor after a period of depression might indicate that the individual has made the decision to end their life.

Changes in Sleep and Appetite

Significant alterations in sleep patterns and appetite can also serve as warning signs of suicidal tendencies:

1. Insomnia or Hypersomnia: Frequent insomnia or excessive sleepiness can indicate an underlying mental health issue and an increased risk of suicide.

2. Changes in Appetite: Noticeable changes in eating habits, such as loss of appetite or excessive overeating, may be indicative of emotional distress.

Recklessness and Risky Behavior

Engaging in reckless activities, without regard for personal safety or consequences, can be a sign of self-destructive tendencies:

1. Substance Abuse: Increased use of drugs or alcohol can be both a coping mechanism and a warning sign of suicidal thoughts.

2. Impulsive Behavior: Engaging in impulsive actions, such as reckless driving or taking unnecessary risks, may reflect a desire to escape from emotional pain.

Social and Emotional Withdrawal

Individuals at risk of suicide often isolate themselves from friends, family, and society as a whole:

1. Loss of Interest: Losing interest in activities that were once enjoyable, such as hobbies or socializing, may be indicative of suicidal thoughts.

2. Withdrawing from Relationships: Suicidal individuals may gradually distance themselves from their loved ones, avoiding contact or canceling plans.

Conclusion

Recognizing the warning signs of suicide is crucial for identifying at-risk individuals and providing timely support. Changes in behavior and mood, verbal and non-verbal cues, alterations in sleep and appetite, reckless behavior, and social withdrawal are all potential indicators of suicidal ideation. If you notice these signs in someone you know or in yourself, it is essential to take them seriously and seek professional help. Remember, intervention and support can save lives, and it is our collective responsibility to address this global mental health crisis.

Introduction

Suicide is a tragic and complex issue that affects millions of people worldwide. It is a leading cause of death, and understanding its underlying factors is crucial for prevention and intervention efforts. Substance abuse, including the misuse of alcohol and drugs, has been closely linked to suicide. This article explores the role of substance abuse in suicide, examining the relationship between these two significant public health concerns.

Substance Abuse and Suicide: The Connection

Substance abuse and suicide often go hand in hand, with one influencing the other in a cyclical pattern. While not all individuals who struggle with substance abuse will contemplate or attempt suicide, research consistently shows a higher prevalence of suicidal thoughts and behaviors among those with substance use disorders.

1. The Prevalence of Substance Abuse in Suicidal Individuals

(a) Statistics on Substance Abuse and Suicide

Cohort studies and surveys have provided compelling evidence of the link between substance abuse and suicide. According to the National Institute on Drug Abuse (NIDA), individuals with substance use disorders are up to six times more likely to die by suicide than those without such disorders.

Alcohol misuse is a significant risk factor for suicidal ideation and attempts. Alcohol's depressive effects on the central nervous system can exacerbate emotional distress, impair judgment, and reduce inhibitions, making individuals more susceptible to impulsive and dangerous behaviors.

Substance abuse often co-occurs with mental health disorders, such as depression, anxiety, and bipolar disorder. These mental health conditions can contribute to feelings of hopelessness, despair, and suicidal thoughts.

Individuals struggling with mental health issues may turn to substance abuse as a form of self-medication or escape from emotional pain. Unfortunately, this coping mechanism can further exacerbate the underlying problems and increase the risk of suicide.

The Mechanisms: How Substance Abuse Increases Suicide Risk

Chronic substance abuse can impair cognitive function, affecting an individual's ability to make sound decisions and solve problems effectively. These deficits can contribute to a sense of hopelessness and a perceived lack of alternatives, potentially increasing the risk of suicidal behavior.

2. Social Isolation and Lack of Support

Substance abuse often leads to social isolation as individuals prioritize drug or alcohol use over interpersonal relationships. This isolation can diminish the availability of support systems, leaving individuals feeling lonely and disconnected, which can exacerbate suicidal ideation.

3. Increased Impulsivity and Aggression

Substance abuse can heighten impulsivity and aggression, leading to impulsive acts of self-harm or violence towards others. These impulsive behaviors, coupled with impaired judgment, can significantly increase the risk of suicide.

Treatment and Prevention Strategies

Addressing substance abuse is crucial for preventing suicide and promoting overall mental health. Effective treatment and prevention strategies should consider the complex interplay between substance abuse and suicidal behaviors.

1. Integrated Treatment Approaches

Integrating mental health and substance abuse treatment is essential for individuals struggling with both issues. This approach involves addressing both conditions simultaneously, as untreated substance abuse can hinder progress in treating mental health disorders and vice versa.

2. Screening and Early Intervention

Screening for substance abuse and suicidal ideation is critical in various settings, including healthcare facilities, schools, and workplaces. Early identification allows for timely intervention and access to appropriate treatment options.

3. Community Support and Education

Raising awareness about the link between substance abuse and suicide is crucial for reducing stigma and encouraging community support. Education programs can promote understanding, empathy, and the availability of resources for individuals at risk.

4. Accessible Mental Health and Addiction Services

Improved access to mental health and addiction services is vital for individuals struggling with substance abuse and suicidal thoughts. Expanding treatment options, reducing barriers, and increasing funding for prevention and intervention programs can save lives.

Conclusion

Substance abuse plays a significant role in suicide, exacerbating risk factors and increasing the likelihood of suicidal thoughts and behaviors. Understanding the complex relationship between substance abuse and suicide is essential for prevention efforts and the development of effective intervention strategies. By addressing substance abuse, integrating treatment approaches, and providing support and education, we can make significant strides in reducing the devastating impact of substance abuse-related suicides and saving lives.

Introduction

Suicide is a tragic and devastating act that claims the lives of far too many adolescents and young adults around the world. The loss of a young life not only affects the individual's family and friends but also leaves a lasting impact on society as a whole. Understanding the factors that contribute to suicide in this age group is crucial for prevention efforts. This article delves into the topic of suicide in adolescents and young adults, examining its prevalence, risk factors, warning signs, and prevention strategies.

Prevalence of Suicide in Adolescents and Young Adults

Suicide is a significant public health concern, particularly among adolescents and young adults. According to the World Health Organization, suicide is the second leading cause of death in individuals aged 15 to 29 years. The statistics are alarming, emphasizing the urgent need to address this issue effectively.

Risk Factors

Several risk factors contribute to the vulnerability of adolescents and young adults to suicidal thoughts and behaviors. Understanding these risk factors can help identify individuals who may be at higher risk and intervene before it's too late. Some common risk factors include:

1. Mental Health Conditions

Mental health disorders, such as depression, anxiety, bipolar disorder, and substance abuse, significantly increase the risk of suicide. Adolescents and young adults experiencing these conditions may struggle with feelings of hopelessness and despair, making them more susceptible to suicidal ideation.

2. History of Suicide Attempts

Individuals with a history of previous suicide attempts are at a higher risk of subsequent attempts. It is essential to provide adequate support and treatment for those who have previously attempted suicide to prevent further incidents.

3. Family History of Suicide

A family history of suicide or a parent who has attempted or completed suicide can increase the likelihood of suicidal behavior in adolescents and young adults. Genetic and environmental factors may contribute to this increased risk.

4. Social Isolation and Loneliness

Feeling disconnected from peers, family, and society can lead to a sense of isolation and loneliness, which can amplify the risk of suicide. Lack of social support systems and difficulties in forming meaningful relationships can contribute to this risk.

Warning Signs

Recognizing the warning signs of suicidal ideation is vital for early intervention. While these signs may vary from person to person, some common indicators include:

Expressions of hopelessness, worthlessness, or a desire to die should never be taken lightly. Statements such as "I can't take it anymore" or "I wish I wasn't here" may indicate suicidal thoughts.

Sudden changes in behavior, such as withdrawal from friends and family, loss of interest in activities once enjoyed, increased irritability, or reckless behavior, can be red flags for potential suicide risk.

Intense emotional distress, frequent mood swings, persistent sadness, or extreme anxiety can be signs of underlying mental health issues that may contribute to suicidal thoughts.

Prevention Strategies

Preventing suicide among adolescents and young adults requires a comprehensive approach that addresses the multiple factors influencing suicidal behavior. Some effective prevention strategies include:

Promoting mental health education and awareness in schools and communities can help reduce the stigma surrounding mental health and encourage individuals to seek help when needed. Educating young people about coping skills and available resources can empower them to manage their mental well-being.

2. Access to Mental Health Services

Improving access to mental health services is crucial. This includes enhancing mental health support within schools, increasing the availability of affordable counseling services, and ensuring comprehensive mental health coverage under healthcare systems.

3. Strong Support Networks

Developing strong support networks within families, schools, and communities can provide a protective factor against suicide. Encouraging open communication and creating safe spaces for individuals to express their feelings can make a significant difference in preventing suicide.

4. Crisis Helplines and Online Resources

Establishing accessible crisis helplines and online resources can provide immediate support to individuals in distress. These services should be widely publicized to ensure that those in need can easily reach out for help.

Conclusion

Suicide among adolescents and young adults is a grave concern that requires urgent attention and collective efforts. By understanding the prevalence, risk factors, warning signs, and implementing effective prevention strategies, we can work towards reducing suicide rates in this vulnerable population. It is crucial to prioritize mental health support, provide accessible resources, and foster a culture of empathy, understanding, and support to save precious lives and build a healthier society for our youth.

Introduction

Suicide is a pressing public health concern that affects individuals of all age groups, including the elderly population. While discussions on suicide often focus on younger demographics, it is crucial to shed light on the unique challenges faced by older adults. As people age, they may encounter various physical, social, and psychological changes that increase their vulnerability to suicidal ideation and behaviors. This article aims to explore these unique challenges and discuss strategies to address and prevent suicide among the elderly.

The Rising Concern of Elderly Suicide

The prevalence and impact of suicide in the elderly population cannot be ignored. Studies have shown that older adults have higher suicide rates compared to other age groups, with the highest rates observed in men over the age of 85. Suicide among the elderly has a significant impact not only on the individuals themselves but also on their families and communities. It is therefore essential to prioritize suicide prevention efforts among older adults.

Physical Health and Suicidal Vulnerability

Physical health conditions and chronic illnesses can contribute to an increased risk of suicidal ideation in the elderly. The burden of chronic pain, disability, and functional decline can significantly impact their mental well-being. Physical health issues should not be overlooked when assessing suicide risk in older adults, and appropriate medical care and support should be provided to address these challenges.

Social Isolation and Loneliness

Social isolation and loneliness are prevalent among the elderly and have detrimental effects on their mental health. As individuals age, they may experience the loss of social support systems, such as the death of a spouse or close friends, leading to increased feelings of loneliness and isolation. These factors contribute to a higher risk of suicidal thoughts and behaviors. Promoting social connections and community engagement can serve as protective factors and help mitigate the risk of suicide among the elderly.

Bereavement and Grief

The grieving process in older adults can be particularly challenging and may contribute to an increased risk of suicide. Significant losses, such as the death of a spouse or close friends, can have a profound impact on an individual's mental well-being. Providing bereavement support and counseling services tailored to the needs of older adults can help mitigate suicide risk during the grieving process.

Mental Health Challenges

Mental health disorders are highly prevalent among the elderly population. Conditions such as depression, anxiety, and cognitive decline can increase the risk of suicide. However, mental health issues in older adults often go undiagnosed and untreated. It is essential to prioritize mental health screening, diagnosis, and treatment in this population to prevent suicide.

Barriers to Seeking Help

Stigma surrounding mental health issues in older adults can act as a significant barrier to seeking help. Many elderly individuals may hesitate to discuss their mental health concerns due to societal attitudes or fear of being labeled as "crazy" or "weak." Moreover, limited access to mental health services and age-related barriers, such as mobility issues or transportation difficulties, further impede older adults from seeking the support they need. Addressing these barriers through education, destigmatization efforts, and improving access to mental health care is crucial.

Enhancing Protective Factors

Identifying and strengthening protective factors is key to preventing suicide among the elderly. Promoting resilience, self-esteem, and a sense of purpose in life can serve as protective factors against suicidal ideation. Encouraging healthy coping mechanisms and positive social interactions can also contribute to the overall well-being of older adults.

Building Supportive Environments

Creating age-friendly communities is vital to support the mental health of older adults. These communities should prioritize social connectedness, provide accessible mental health services tailored to older adults' needs, and ensure adequate support for caregivers. Educating caregivers, healthcare professionals, and community members on recognizing and addressing suicide risk in the elderly is essential in building a supportive environment.

Collaboration and Integrated Care

Suicide prevention efforts for the elderly require interdisciplinary collaboration and integrated care. Mental health services should be integrated into primary care settings, as primary care providers often have regular contact with older adults. Establishing referral systems and coordination between healthcare providers can ensure comprehensive care for older adults at risk of suicide.

Conclusion

Suicide among the elderly is a complex issue that demands attention and proactive interventions. By understanding the unique challenges faced by older adults, such as physical health issues, social isolation, bereavement, and mental health struggles, we can develop effective prevention strategies. Through collaboration, education, and improved access to care, we can work towards reducing the rates of suicide in the elderly and ensuring a healthier and more fulfilling life for our seniors.

Introduction

Suicide is a deeply distressing issue that affects individuals across all demographics, but within the LGBTQ+ community, it poses a particularly significant concern. LGBTQ+ individuals often face unique challenges and societal pressures that can contribute to higher rates of suicide. In this article, we will delve into the factors contributing to the alarming suicide rates among the LGBTQ+ community, explore the impact of discrimination and stigma, discuss mental health disparities, and highlight the importance of support and acceptance.

Understanding the Context

1. Defining the LGBTQ+ Community

The LGBTQ+ community encompasses individuals who identify as lesbian, gay, bisexual, transgender, queer, or other sexual orientations and gender identities. It is a diverse group with distinct experiences and challenges.

2. Prevalence of Suicide

Studies consistently indicate that LGBTQ+ individuals are at a higher risk of suicidal ideation, attempts, and completed suicides compared to their heterosexual and cisgender counterparts.

Contributing Factors

1. Discrimination and Stigma

Social Stigma: Widespread prejudice and discrimination can lead to feelings of rejection, isolation, and shame among LGBTQ+ individuals.

Family Rejection: Experiencing rejection or lack of acceptance from family members can significantly impact mental health and increase suicide risk.

Bullying and Harassment: LGBTQ+ youth often face bullying and harassment at school or in their communities, which can have detrimental effects on their mental well-being.

2. Mental Health Disparities

Minority Stress: The cumulative effects of discrimination, stigma, and marginalization can contribute to minority stress, leading to higher rates of mental health disorders.

Internalized Homophobia and Transphobia: Internalized negative beliefs about one's sexual orientation or gender identity can contribute to self-hatred and increased risk of suicide.

Promoting Mental Health and Resilience

1. Access to Affirmative Mental Health Care

Culturally Competent Providers: Training mental health professionals to understand the unique challenges faced by LGBTQ+ individuals is crucial.

Safe Spaces: Creating safe and inclusive environments where individuals can seek mental health support without fear of judgment or discrimination.

2. Peer Support and Community Engagement

LGBTQ+ Support Groups: Peer support groups can provide a sense of belonging and understanding for individuals struggling with their mental health.

Community Organizations: Organizations and initiatives that focus on LGBTQ+ mental health can provide valuable resources, education, and advocacy.

3. Education and Awareness

Schools and Institutions: Implementing comprehensive anti-bullying policies and inclusive curricula can foster acceptance and reduce the risk of suicide among LGBTQ+ youth.

Media Representation: Promoting positive and accurate representation of LGBTQ+ individuals in the media can help combat stereotypes and reduce stigma.

Creating a Supportive Society

1. Policy and Legal Reforms

Anti-Discrimination Laws: Implementing comprehensive anti-discrimination laws can protect the rights of LGBTQ+ individuals in employment, housing, and public services.

Conversion Therapy Bans: Banning harmful conversion therapy practices that aim to change an individual's sexual orientation or gender identity.

2. Allyship and Acceptance

Supportive Families: Family acceptance and support play a crucial role in the mental well-being of LGBTQ+ individuals.

Intersectionality: Recognizing and addressing the intersecting identities and experiences within the LGBTQ+ community can foster a more inclusive and supportive environment.

Conclusion

The alarmingly high rates of suicide within the LGBTQ+ community demand urgent attention and action. By addressing the factors contributing to these disparities, promoting mental health care, fostering acceptance, and implementing inclusive policies, we can work towards reducing suicide rates and creating a society where all individuals, regardless of sexual orientation or gender identity, can thrive. It is essential for everyone to contribute to a world that embraces diversity and supports the well-being of every member of the LGBTQ+ community.

Introduction

Suicide is a pressing public health concern worldwide, and the military is no exception to this tragic reality. In recent years, the military has grappled with an alarming increase in suicide rates among service members. Understanding the unique risk factors associated with military service is crucial in developing effective prevention strategies and providing much-needed support to those who serve. This article explores the distinctive challenges faced by military personnel and the strategies needed to address and mitigate the risk factors contributing to suicide.

The Impact of Combat Exposure

Combat exposure is one of the most significant risk factors for suicide in the military. Service members who have experienced intense combat situations may suffer from post-traumatic stress disorder (PTSD), depression, and other mental health conditions, increasing their vulnerability to suicidal ideation. The trauma of war can have long-lasting effects on an individual's mental well-being, making it essential to provide comprehensive mental health support to those who have been exposed to combat.

Transition and Reintegration

Transitioning from military to civilian life can be a challenging process, creating a period of vulnerability for service members. The abrupt change in routine, loss of camaraderie, and difficulties in finding employment can contribute to feelings of isolation and despair. Adequate support systems and resources must be in place to assist service members during this critical transition phase and help them reintegrate into society successfully.

Stigma and Barriers to Seeking Help

Stigma surrounding mental health issues persists within the military culture, making it difficult for service members to seek help when they need it most. The fear of being perceived as weak or lacking resilience often prevents individuals from reaching out for support. It is crucial to foster a culture that promotes open discussions about mental health, reduces the associated stigma, and encourages service members to seek assistance without fear of judgment or retribution.

Access to Lethal Means

The military environment inherently provides access to lethal means, such as firearms and explosives. This accessibility increases the risk of impulsive acts and exacerbates the potential for completed suicides. Implementing strict safety protocols, including secure storage of weapons and ammunition, can help mitigate this risk factor and prevent impulsive actions during moments of crisis.

Substance Abuse and Co-occurring Disorders

Substance abuse and co-occurring mental health disorders are prevalent risk factors for suicide among military personnel. The stressors of military life, coupled with the unique challenges faced during deployment, can contribute to the development of substance abuse disorders. It is crucial to provide comprehensive substance abuse treatment programs and mental health services that address co-occurring disorders to ensure service members receive the necessary support for their well-being.

Family and Relationship Strain

Military service can place significant strain on familial and personal relationships. Lengthy deployments, frequent relocations, and the overall demands of military life can lead to feelings of isolation and disconnection. Building robust support networks for military families and providing marriage and family counseling services can help alleviate relationship strain and reduce the risk of suicide among service members.

Leadership and Command Climate

The leadership and command climate within the military play a vital role in addressing suicide risk factors. Leaders must prioritize mental health and create an environment that encourages help-seeking behaviors. Implementing training programs for leaders on recognizing and responding to mental health concerns can ensure that service members receive the necessary support at every level of command.

Enhanced Mental Health Screening

Early identification of mental health concerns is crucial in preventing suicide. Implementing regular mental health screenings throughout a service member's career can help identify individuals who may be at increased risk. These screenings can serve as an opportunity for early intervention, ensuring that appropriate resources and support are provided to those in need.

Conclusion

Suicide in the military remains a critical issue that requires a multifaceted approach. By recognizing and addressing the unique risk factors faced by military personnel, we can develop targeted prevention strategies and provide effective support systems. Combating stigma, improving access to mental health care, and fostering resilient leadership are essential steps in reducing the incidence of suicide among those who selflessly serve their country. With concerted efforts, we can work towards a military environment that prioritizes the well-being of its members and ensures they receive the support they need to thrive.

Introduction

In today's digital age, where technology has become an integral part of our lives, the issue of cyberbullying has emerged as a serious concern. With the increasing use of social media platforms, online forums, and messaging apps, individuals, particularly young people, are vulnerable to the harmful effects of cyberbullying. One devastating consequence of cyberbullying is the connection it has with suicide. This article aims to explore the relationship between cyberbullying and suicide, shedding light on the impact it has on individuals' mental health and well-being.

Understanding Cyberbullying

Cyberbullying refers to the act of using digital communication tools to harass, intimidate, or harm someone. Unlike traditional bullying, cyberbullying takes place online, making it easier for bullies to hide their identities and reach their victims anytime, anywhere. This form of bullying can manifest in various ways, including sending threatening or hateful messages, spreading rumors, sharing private information, or posting humiliating content. The anonymous nature of the internet often emboldens perpetrators, making cyberbullying an insidious problem.

The Effects of Cyberbullying

The impact of cyberbullying on victims is profound and can have long-lasting consequences. Constant exposure to online harassment can lead to significant psychological distress, including anxiety, depression, low self-esteem, and feelings of isolation. Victims may experience difficulties in concentrating on their studies or work, leading to academic or professional setbacks. Moreover, cyberbullying can permeate all aspects of a person's life, making it difficult to escape the torment even within the safety of their own homes.

The Link to Suicide

Tragically, there is a strong association between cyberbullying and suicide. The relentless nature of online harassment, coupled with the inability to escape from it, can push individuals to their breaking point. For some victims, the emotional pain becomes unbearable, leading to thoughts of self-harm or suicide as a means to escape their torment. Several studies have shown a clear correlation between cyberbullying victimization and suicidal ideation, attempts, and completed suicides. It is crucial to recognize the severity of this issue and take proactive measures to prevent such tragic outcomes.

Contributing Factors

Several factors contribute to the connection between cyberbullying and suicide. First, the anonymity provided by the internet often emboldens bullies, as they can harass their victims without facing immediate consequences. This lack of accountability increases the intensity and frequency of cyberbullying incidents. Additionally, the widespread reach of social media platforms allows harmful content to spread rapidly, amplifying its impact on victims. The 24/7 accessibility of technology further intensifies the harassment, as victims are constantly reminded of the abuse they endure.

Prevention and Intervention Strategies

Addressing cyberbullying requires a multi-faceted approach involving various stakeholders, including parents, educators, policymakers, and online platforms. Here are some strategies that can help prevent and intervene in cases of cyberbullying:

1. Education and Awareness: Promote education campaigns that raise awareness about cyberbullying, its consequences, and strategies for prevention. This includes teaching young people how to be responsible digital citizens and promoting empathy and respect online.

2. Parental Involvement: Encourage parents to monitor their children's online activities, establish open lines of communication, and provide guidance on internet safety. Parental involvement plays a crucial role in detecting signs of cyberbullying and providing necessary support.

3. School Policies and Support: Schools should implement strict anti-cyberbullying policies, providing clear guidelines on reporting incidents and consequences for perpetrators. Additionally, schools can offer counseling services and safe spaces for victims to seek support.

4. Online Platform Responsibility: Social media platforms and online communities must take a proactive stance against cyberbullying. This includes developing effective reporting systems, swift action against offenders, and implementing algorithms to detect and remove harmful content.

Conclusion

The link between cyberbullying and suicide highlights the urgent need to address this issue. By understanding the profound impact of cyberbullying on victims' mental health and well-being, we can work towards creating a safer and more inclusive digital environment. Through education, awareness, and collaborative efforts, we can prevent cyberbullying and provide support to those affected. It is only by standing together against cyberbullying that we can protect vulnerable individuals and save lives.

Introduction

The COVID-19 pandemic has significantly impacted various aspects of society, including mental health. While the virus itself poses physical health risks, the measures taken to control its spread have resulted in significant social and economic consequences. One such consequence is the potential impact on suicide rates worldwide. This article aims to explore the relationship between the COVID-19 pandemic and suicide rates, offering a global perspective on this concerning issue.

The COVID-19 Pandemic and Mental Health

The COVID-19 pandemic has created a perfect storm for mental health challenges. The fear of contracting the virus, social isolation, economic instability, and disruptions in daily life have all contributed to increased stress, anxiety, and depression among individuals worldwide. These factors play a crucial role in understanding the potential impact on suicide rates.

Economic Downturn and Suicide Rates

The economic downturn resulting from the pandemic has been a significant contributor to increased suicide rates. Job losses, business closures, and financial strain have heightened feelings of hopelessness and despair for many individuals. Unemployment rates and financial stress have historically been linked to higher suicide rates, emphasizing the need for comprehensive support systems during times of crisis.

Social Isolation and Loneliness

Strict lockdown measures and social distancing guidelines have led to increased social isolation and loneliness among people of all ages. Humans are inherently social beings, and prolonged isolation can have severe psychological consequences. Studies have shown that social isolation is a significant risk factor for suicide, as individuals lack the social support networks that provide a sense of belonging and emotional well-being.

Access to Mental Health Services

The COVID-19 pandemic has strained healthcare systems globally, resulting in reduced access to mental health services. Overwhelmed hospitals and clinics, limited resources, and a shift in focus towards managing the virus have hindered individuals' ability to seek and receive appropriate mental health care. The lack of accessible and affordable mental health services can have dire consequences for those struggling with their mental well-being.

Vulnerable Populations

Certain populations have been disproportionately affected by the pandemic, leading to increased suicide risks. This includes frontline healthcare workers, who face immense pressure and emotional distress, as well as individuals with pre-existing mental health conditions. Additionally, children and adolescents have experienced disruptions in their education, socialization, and support systems, putting them at an increased risk of mental health challenges.

Regional Variations in Suicide Rates

The impact of the COVID-19 pandemic on suicide rates varies across different regions. Factors such as cultural norms, healthcare infrastructure, government response, and public health measures influence the magnitude of this impact. While some countries have reported an increase in suicide rates, others have not seen a significant change. Comprehensive data collection and analysis are essential to understand the nuances and develop targeted interventions.

Mitigating the Impact

Addressing the impact of COVID-19 on suicide rates requires a multi-faceted approach. Governments and healthcare systems must prioritize mental health services and ensure their accessibility to all individuals, especially the most vulnerable. Implementing public health measures that balance physical and mental well-being is crucial. Additionally, raising awareness about mental health, reducing stigma, and fostering social connections are vital to mitigating the impact of the pandemic on suicide rates.

Conclusion

The COVID-19 pandemic has presented a global mental health crisis, with potential implications for suicide rates worldwide. The economic downturn, social isolation, limited access to mental health services, and the vulnerability of certain populations have exacerbated mental health challenges. To address this issue, a comprehensive response is necessary, focusing on providing support, expanding mental health services, and promoting overall well-being. By prioritizing mental health in the recovery process, societies can help mitigate the impact of the pandemic on suicide rates and ensure the well-being of individuals around the world.

Introduction

Suicide is a tragic and complex event that not only affects the person who takes their own life but also leaves a lasting impact on their family and friends. The aftermath of suicide is characterized by a range of emotions and challenges that can be overwhelming for those left behind. This article aims to explore the profound impact of suicide on the loved ones of the deceased, shedding light on the emotional, psychological, and social repercussions they experience.

Initial Shock and Disbelief

When a loved one dies by suicide, family and friends often find themselves in a state of profound shock and disbelief. The sudden and unexpected nature of suicide can make it incredibly difficult to process and accept. They may struggle to comprehend why the person chose to end their own life, grappling with a mix of intense emotions such as guilt, anger, and sadness.

Emotional Turmoil and Grief

The loss of a loved one to suicide triggers a unique and complex form of grief. Survivors often experience a rollercoaster of emotions, ranging from profound sadness and emptiness to anger and confusion. They may struggle with feelings of guilt, questioning whether they missed signs or could have done more to prevent the suicide. The grief process is further complicated by the stigma associated with suicide, which can lead to feelings of shame or isolation.

Sense of Abandonment and Rejection

For family and friends, suicide can evoke a deep sense of abandonment and rejection. They may wonder why their loved one chose to leave them behind, feeling a void that can be hard to fill. The feelings of rejection can be particularly challenging to reconcile, as survivors struggle to make sense of their relationship with the deceased and may grapple with unresolved issues.

Mental Health Impact

The impact of suicide extends beyond grief and emotional distress, often taking a toll on the mental health of those left behind. Survivors may experience a range of mental health issues, such as depression, anxiety, post-traumatic stress disorder (PTSD), and suicidal ideation. Witnessing or discovering the aftermath of a suicide can traumatize loved ones, exacerbating their vulnerability to mental health challenges.

Social Stigma and Isolation

The stigma surrounding suicide can lead to social isolation for the family and friends of the deceased. Society's misconceptions and judgments about suicide often result in avoidance or judgment, making it difficult for survivors to find support and understanding. This isolation can further exacerbate feelings of grief, shame, and guilt, leaving individuals feeling misunderstood and alone.

Disrupted Relationships and Family Dynamics

The aftermath of suicide can disrupt relationships and family dynamics in profound ways. Family members and friends may experience strained relationships as they grapple with their own emotions and try to navigate their grief together. The loss can strain marriages, friendships, and other relationships as each individual copes with the aftermath in their own way.

Increased Risk of Suicide

Tragically, the suicide of a loved one can increase the risk of suicide among survivors. Individuals who have lost someone to suicide are at a higher risk of experiencing suicidal thoughts or engaging in self-destructive behaviors. This underscores the importance of providing appropriate support and resources to help those affected by suicide cope with their grief and reduce the risk of further tragedy.

Conclusion

The impact of suicide on family and friends is profound and far-reaching, encompassing emotional, psychological, and social dimensions. Understanding the unique challenges faced by survivors can help promote empathy, support, and effective interventions to mitigate the long-term effects. It is crucial to foster an open dialogue about suicide, reduce stigma, and provide resources and mental health services to both the immediate survivors and the wider community. By acknowledging the impact of suicide on family and friends, we can work towards creating a more compassionate and supportive environment for those affected by this tragic loss.

Introduction

Suicide is a global public health concern, and its impact on individuals, families, and communities cannot be underestimated. However, it is a preventable tragedy, and there are various strategies and resources available to address this issue. In this article, we will explore effective suicide prevention programs and resources that aim to identify at-risk individuals, provide support, and ultimately save lives.

Understanding Suicide: A Complex Issue

Before delving into prevention strategies, it is crucial to understand the complexity of suicide. Suicide is often the result of a combination of factors, including mental health disorders, substance abuse, social isolation, financial stress, and previous suicide attempts. Recognizing the risk factors and warning signs associated with suicidal behavior is essential for effective prevention.

Gatekeeper Training: Empowering Communities

One crucial strategy for suicide prevention is gatekeeper training. Gatekeepers are individuals in positions of influence, such as teachers, coaches, and community leaders, who can identify and assist at-risk individuals. Various evidence-based training programs, such as Applied Suicide Intervention Skills Training (ASIST) and Question, Persuade, Refer (QPR), equip gatekeepers with the knowledge and skills to recognize warning signs, engage in a conversation about suicide, and connect individuals to appropriate resources.

Crisis Hotlines: A Lifeline in Times of Distress

Crisis hotlines play a vital role in suicide prevention by providing immediate support to individuals in crisis. These hotlines, often staffed by trained volunteers and mental health professionals, offer a confidential and empathetic ear to those struggling with suicidal thoughts. Notable crisis hotlines include the National Suicide Prevention Lifeline in the United States and organizations like Samaritans in the United Kingdom. These helplines are available 24/7, providing a lifeline for individuals in their darkest moments.

Mental Health Screening and Assessment

Identifying individuals at risk of suicide can be challenging, but mental health screening and assessment tools can help in early detection. Screening tools like the Patient Health Questionnaire (PHQ-9) and the Columbia-Suicide Severity Rating Scale (C-SSRS) aid in identifying individuals who may be experiencing depression, anxiety, or suicidal ideation. These assessments enable healthcare professionals to intervene promptly and provide appropriate treatment and support.

School-Based Programs: Nurturing Resilience

Given that many suicidal individuals are young, implementing suicide prevention programs in schools is crucial. These programs focus on building resilience, promoting mental health awareness, and providing early intervention. Programs such as Signs of Suicide (SOS) and

Sources of Strength engage students, educators, and parents in discussions about mental health, destigmatize seeking help, and teach coping skills. By fostering a supportive and inclusive environment, schools can play a vital role in preventing suicide among young people.

Collaborative Care: Integrating Mental and Physical Health

Collaborative care models bring together primary care providers, mental health professionals, and other specialists to provide comprehensive care for individuals at risk of suicide. By integrating mental health services into primary care settings, collaborative care models ensure a holistic approach to suicide prevention. These programs facilitate early detection, coordination of treatment, and ongoing support, improving outcomes for individuals with mental health concerns.

Postvention: Supporting Survivors

After a suicide occurs, it is crucial to provide support to those left behind, known as survivors of suicide loss. Postvention strategies aim to help survivors navigate the grieving process, access resources, and reduce the risk of subsequent suicides. Support groups, counseling services, and educational resources help survivors cope with the loss and promote healing within the community.

Conclusion

Suicide prevention requires a multifaceted approach, involving community engagement, access to mental health resources, and early intervention. By implementing effective programs and utilizing available resources, we can work towards reducing the incidence of suicide and providing support to those in need. Together, we can create a world where individuals facing crisis find hope, understanding, and the help they deserve. Remember, every life matters, and through collective efforts, we can make a difference.

Introduction

Suicide is a global public health concern that claims the lives of millions of individuals every year. It is a complex issue influenced by various factors, including mental health conditions. Mental health professionals play a crucial role in suicide prevention by providing essential support, assessment, intervention, and treatment to individuals at risk. This article explores the significant role mental health professionals play in suicide prevention and highlights their contributions in saving lives.

Understanding the Scope of the Problem

Suicide rates have been rising steadily worldwide, emphasizing the need for effective prevention strategies. Mental health professionals are at the forefront of addressing this crisis. They possess the necessary expertise to identify risk factors and warning signs associated with suicidal ideation. By understanding the complexity of mental health conditions and risk factors, these professionals can assess individuals' vulnerability to suicide accurately.

Early Detection and Assessment

One of the primary roles of mental health professionals in suicide prevention is early detection and assessment. They are trained to recognize signs of distress, such as changes in behavior, mood, or social interactions. Through comprehensive evaluations, mental health professionals can identify individuals at risk and develop appropriate intervention plans. Their expertise enables them to differentiate between temporary distress and severe suicidal ideation, allowing for timely and targeted interventions.

Crisis Intervention and Support

During moments of crisis, mental health professionals provide essential support to individuals experiencing suicidal thoughts. They offer a safe and non-judgmental environment where individuals can express their emotions openly. By actively listening and demonstrating empathy, mental health professionals establish rapport and trust, fostering a therapeutic relationship. Through crisis intervention techniques, they can help individuals explore alternative coping strategies and provide immediate support when it is needed most.

Development of Safety Plans

Mental health professionals play a vital role in developing safety plans for individuals at risk of suicide. These plans outline steps to be taken during moments of crisis, including identifying support networks, coping mechanisms, and emergency contacts. By collaboratively creating safety plans, mental health professionals empower individuals to actively participate in their own well-being and provide them with tangible tools to manage suicidal thoughts effectively.

Psychotherapy and Treatment

Therapy and treatment form the core of mental health professionals' interventions in suicide prevention. They employ evidence-based psychotherapeutic approaches tailored to individuals' needs, such as cognitive-behavioral therapy (CBT), dialectical behavior therapy (DBT), and psychodynamic therapy. These therapies aim to address underlying mental health issues, develop coping skills, and enhance resilience. By providing ongoing treatment and support, mental health professionals play a crucial role in preventing relapses and promoting long-term well-being.

Collaboration with Other Healthcare Providers

Collaboration among healthcare providers is vital in suicide prevention efforts. Mental health professionals work in tandem with primary care physicians, psychiatrists, and other specialists to ensure comprehensive care for individuals at risk. Through coordinated efforts, they facilitate information sharing, establish treatment plans, and monitor progress. This collaborative approach maximizes the effectiveness of interventions and enhances the overall support system available to individuals struggling with suicidal ideation.

Public Education and Awareness

Mental health professionals actively contribute to public education and awareness campaigns aimed at reducing the stigma surrounding suicide and mental health conditions. By disseminating accurate information and resources, they help communities understand the signs of distress, promote help-seeking behaviors, and foster supportive environments. Through workshops, presentations, and media engagement, mental health professionals play a crucial role in destigmatizing mental health and encouraging early intervention.

Conclusion

The role of mental health professionals in suicide prevention cannot be overstated. Their expertise in early detection, assessment, crisis intervention, safety planning, psychotherapy, and collaboration with other healthcare providers significantly contributes to saving lives. By actively engaging in public education and awareness initiatives, mental health professionals also play a vital role in preventing suicide on a broader scale. It is crucial to support and prioritize the mental health workforce to ensure that individuals at risk of suicide receive the comprehensive care they need. By doing so, we can foster a society where mental well-being is prioritized and lives are saved.

Introduction

Suicide is a complex and sensitive topic that raises profound ethical questions. The act of intentionally ending one's own life has been a subject of contemplation and debate across different cultures and religions. While attitudes towards suicide vary significantly, examining the cultural and religious perspectives can shed light on the ethical considerations surrounding this deeply personal decision.

Cultural Perspectives on Suicide

1. Western Culture

In Western cultures, suicide is generally regarded as a tragic and avoidable act. The emphasis is placed on the sanctity of life, the importance of preserving it, and the belief in the inherent value and potential for growth even in the face of adversity. Suicide is often seen as a sign of mental distress, and efforts are made to prevent and treat suicidal tendencies through therapy and support systems.

2. Eastern Culture

In contrast, some Eastern cultures, such as Japan, have historically held a more nuanced view of suicide. In Japan, the act of seppuku, a ritualistic form of suicide, was considered an honorable way to preserve one's dignity or to atone for wrongdoing. However, modern attitudes towards suicide in Japan have shifted, with greater emphasis on mental health support and suicide prevention.

Religious Perspectives on Suicide

1. Christianity

Christianity, which encompasses various denominations, generally condemns suicide as a violation of the sanctity of life. The belief in a divine plan and the inherent worth of every individual shapes this perspective. However, interpretations may differ among different Christian denominations, and compassion and understanding are often extended towards those who experience mental anguish.

2. Islam

In Islam, suicide is widely regarded as a grave sin and is strictly prohibited. Muslims believe that life is a gift from Allah and that it is not within human rights to take one's own life. Islamic teachings emphasize patience, seeking help, and relying on faith in times of distress. Suicide prevention and mental health support are seen as crucial in Islamic communities.

3. Buddhism

Buddhism, with its focus on suffering and the impermanence of life, takes a more nuanced stance on suicide. While Buddhism considers suicide an unskillful act that perpetuates suffering, the emphasis is on understanding the causes of suffering and finding liberation from it. Compassion and non-judgmental support are often extended to individuals experiencing mental anguish.

In Hinduism, the perspective on suicide varies depending on different philosophical and cultural traditions. The concept of life and death in Hinduism is deeply intertwined with the belief in reincarnation, the cyclical process of rebirth. Suicide is generally discouraged as it is seen as interrupting one's spiritual journey and creating negative karma, which can have adverse effects on future lives.

However, there are exceptions within Hinduism, especially in the context of certain historical and mythological narratives. For instance, the concept of "sati," where a widow would self-immolate on her husband's funeral pyre, was practiced in certain regions and time periods. This practice, while controversial and largely discontinued, was seen as a way for a widow to demonstrate her devotion and preserve her honor.

In modern Hinduism, suicide is generally considered a tragic act resulting from mental anguish and despair. Hindu teachings emphasize the importance of spiritual growth, self-realization, and the pursuit of dharma (righteousness). Mental health support and compassionate understanding are advocated to prevent and address the underlying causes of suicidal thoughts and behaviors.

Ethical Considerations

1. Autonomy and Personal Freedom

The concept of autonomy, the ability to make decisions based on personal values and beliefs, is central to the ethical considerations surrounding suicide. Supporters argue that individuals should have the right to choose the course of their lives, including the decision to end their suffering. However, opponents highlight the potential consequences, such as the impact on loved ones and the potential for irreversible actions during transient moments of distress.

2. Mental Health and Treatment

The ethical dimensions of suicide also intersect with mental health. Mental illnesses, such as depression and anxiety, can cloud judgment and distort one's perception of reality. Advocates stress the importance of providing accessible mental health care, destigmatizing mental illnesses, and offering supportive environments to prevent suicide and provide alternatives to those in despair.

3. Societal Impact and Prevention

The ripple effects of suicide on families, friends, and communities cannot be ignored. The loss of life through suicide can have lasting emotional and psychological impacts on those left behind. Consequently, suicide prevention strategies, including public awareness campaigns, early intervention, and improved mental health services, are considered ethically imperative to safeguard lives and provide support.

Conclusion

The ethics of suicide are multifaceted, influenced by cultural norms, religious teachings, and individual perspectives. While Western cultures tend to emphasize prevention and support, some Eastern cultures historically held a more complex view. Religions, such as Christianity, Islam, Buddhism, and Hinduism offer unique perspectives on suicide, often emphasizing the sanctity of life or the importance of understanding and compassion. Ultimately, the ethical considerations surrounding suicide call for a delicate balance between personal autonomy, mental health support, and the well-being of individuals and communities as a whole.

Introduction

Suicide is a global public health issue that affects millions of individuals and their families every year. It is a complex and multifaceted problem that requires a comprehensive approach to prevention and awareness. While progress has been made in recent years, there is still much work to be done in order to effectively address this pressing concern. This article explores the importance of moving forward with suicide prevention and awareness, highlighting key strategies and initiatives that can make a difference in saving lives.

Understanding the Scope of the Problem

Before diving into the solutions, it is crucial to understand the scope of the problem. According to the World Health Organization (WHO), close to 800,000 people die by suicide each year, making it the second leading cause of death among individuals aged 15-29. These statistics reflect the urgency of the issue and the need for immediate action.

Breaking the Stigma

One of the major barriers in suicide prevention is the stigma associated with mental health and seeking help. Society must work towards destigmatizing mental health issues and creating an environment where individuals feel safe and supported when discussing their struggles. This can be achieved through public awareness campaigns, education programs, and open conversations about mental health in schools, workplaces, and communities.

Early Intervention and Accessible Resources

Early intervention plays a critical role in suicide prevention. It is essential to identify warning signs and risk factors, such as sudden behavioral changes, social withdrawal, or expressions of hopelessness. Mental health literacy should be promoted to help individuals recognize these signs and provide appropriate support.

Additionally, it is imperative to ensure that mental health resources are easily accessible to those in need. Governments, healthcare organizations, and community groups should collaborate to establish helplines, crisis centers, and affordable mental health services. Investing in mental health infrastructure and training more mental health professionals can make a significant difference in saving lives.

Promoting Mental Health and Resilience

Preventing suicide requires a proactive approach that focuses on promoting mental health and building resilience in individuals. This involves implementing mental health programs in schools, workplaces, and community settings. These programs can provide individuals with the necessary tools and coping mechanisms to navigate life's challenges and develop emotional well-being.

Education and Training

Educating the general public about suicide prevention and mental health is crucial for raising awareness and reducing the stigma surrounding the topic. Mental health literacy should be incorporated into school curricula, equipping students with the knowledge and skills to support themselves and others. Training programs should also be provided to teachers, healthcare professionals, and community leaders, enabling them to identify warning signs and respond effectively.

Collaboration and Partnerships

Addressing suicide prevention requires a collaborative effort involving various stakeholders. Governments, healthcare organizations, non-profit organizations, and community groups must work together to develop comprehensive strategies and initiatives. By pooling resources, sharing best practices, and coordinating efforts, a more cohesive approach can be achieved, maximizing the impact of suicide prevention and awareness initiatives.

Harnessing the Power of Technology

In today's digital age, technology can play a vital role in suicide prevention and awareness. Online platforms and social media can be utilized to disseminate information, provide support, and connect individuals to resources. Technology-based tools such as mobile applications and chatbots can also be developed to offer immediate assistance and guidance to those in crisis.

Conclusion

Moving forward with suicide prevention and awareness is not an option; it is a necessity. By breaking the stigma, promoting mental health, providing accessible resources, and fostering collaboration, we can make a positive impact and save lives. It is essential for governments, organizations, and individuals to come together, prioritize mental health, and work tirelessly towards a world where no one has to suffer in silence. Let us move forward with determination, compassion, and resilience, striving to create a future free from the tragedy of suicide.

"Understanding Suicide: Prevention, Awareness, and Moving Forward" is a comprehensive and insightful book that delves into the complex and sensitive topic of suicide. Through its thoughtfully structured chapters, the book explores various aspects of suicide, including its definition, prevalence, and the crucial link between mental health and suicide. It guides readers through identifying warning signs, risk factors, and the social, cultural, and economic influences that contribute to suicide. The book also addresses specific populations at risk, such as adolescents, the elderly, and the LGBTQ+ community, providing a deep understanding of their unique challenges. Moreover, it explores the impact of suicide on families and friends and offers effective strategies for suicide prevention, including a discussion on the role of mental health professionals and available resources. With chapters dedicated to ethical considerations, the global perspective of COVID-19, and the connection between cyberbullying and suicide, this book provides a comprehensive view of the subject. Ultimately, it aims to foster a greater awareness and understanding of suicide, equipping readers with the knowledge needed to prevent future tragedies and move forward towards a more compassionate and supportive society.

ABOUT THE AUTHOR

Mr. C. P. Kumar is a retired Scientist 'G' from National Institute of Hydrology, Roorkee, Uttarakhand, India. He is also a Reiki Healer and Chakra Balancing practitioner (with pendulum dowsing) and offers Emotional Freedom Technique (EFT) to help individuals with emotional issues. Mr. Kumar has authored many books on technical, spiritual, and social topics.

For further details, you may visit his webpage
https://www.angelfire.com/nh/cpkumar/virgo.html